Spiritual Life, a Journey to Freedom

A True Account of a Working Medium

Laura Payne

||| Clink
Street

London | New York

Published by Clink Street Publishing 2020

ISBN:
978-1-913340-56-8 - paperback
978-1-913340-57-5 - ebook

Contents

Have you ever wondered what it is like to live a life entwined with Spirit and the Spirit world?

*I have delved into and faced
my darkest fears.*

*I have seen my darkest hour, it has been
like a raging storm and it has passed.*

It has taught me;

*To be me, to be kind, to be in control, to
be at peace, to help others.*

To love the Earth and nature.

*To live alongside the magic, with the
magic, use the magic.*

To love, to honour death, to honour life.

*To honour my every waking day and to
honour every time I lay down my head.*

*I am blessed because I accept, I am of
source, I am one with the universe.*

I will be my purpose.

*I will exist to live and live to exist in the
light that I share with my kind.*

I am me.

*In memory of my
beloved Father and
Mother, my greatest
source of inspiration
and strength.*

I grew up on a farm in rural North Warwickshire, England. As a young child and still to this day I have always adored nature, animals and was very aware of the love that surrounded me. I was a happy free spirit with a brave, adventurous side, giving me the family nickname of 'The Wild Child'. My compassionate nature meant that I was popular with girls at school, whilst my adventurous side made me a match for any boy. Suffice to say I had a fantastic childhood and life was a dream and an adventure. Love is the energy of life, in us, in nature and animals and I was very aware of this.

I was always very spiritually open and aware, from a young child I sensed and saw the magic in the trees, the grasses, the corn and the flowers. It was almost like I knew what animals were thinking and feeling and I could get close to animals. I felt the beauty, light and power of the sunshine and the nurturing of the rain and I loved the magic and mystery of the dark night and the cycles of the moon. I would always look out for shooting stars in the unpolluted night sky on the farm and would be sure to make a wish, trusting it to come true.

I always noticed and picked up feathers I found, and still do, symbols of our loved ones in spirit or messages from the angels. Candles were symbolic, a connection to God and his Divine love, not just something pretty and lighting a candle was and still is sacred. I saw the spirit in others and knew of its importance, loyalty and kindness, feeling others pain and wanting to heal them. A gift I have used via touch and prayer my whole life.

My earliest memory of seeing spirit as beings is as a toddler. I would be in awe of the spirits around me and never concentrated on the adults, to the point that they thought I was deaf and I was taken for a hearing test. As a child I would go to bed and as soon as my parent had left the room and I was beginning to drop off to sleep, I would sense activity in my bedroom. Tugging at my sheet and trying to get my attention. This happened every night and kept me awake. I saw a white light of a young girl and then I began to receive information. I named her Annie and she was no older than me. I learnt that she had died from an illness in that house many years ago and that she just wanted to play with me.

I wasn't scared though I was struggling to get off to sleep and I complained to my mother. She didn't seem surprised instead asked our vicar to come. My family stood holding hands in a circle whilst the vicar asked the spirit to move on to the next life. Before Annie left, I saw her through my window. One last goodbye. She didn't return to visit me until many years later, though by then I was well trained myself and would not tolerate 2 am chats. However, I did acknowledge her and I knew she was only popping in to say hi.

When I was eight years old, I had a hamster, a tiny golden hamster from Martins Pet Shop. I named her Martini, but not after the drink! I loved her dearly and she lived to be a remarkable age of almost five years rare for any hamster. When she finally passed, I longed to see her just one more time. I asked Divine God, begged him. Then one night I saw a golden light, Martini my spirit hamster. The light was of a hamster shape, she was free and ran across my floor. A true miracle.

Also around this age, I remember my mum had a child's jumper in her bedroom for months. One day she said, 'I just don't know who's this is.' We always had lots of children round to play. I held the jumper and I smelt it I instantly knew which child's it was. It could have been one of many and I told mum. She made a phone call and sure enough it was the child's whom I had named. Mum was both baffled yet greatly relieved that the jumper was now returned to its rightful owner.

As I entered high school my psychic senses grew stronger and I could suss people out by only having to be near them. At this time my father was very wary of spiritual practises and I was not encouraged to attend a spiritual church or learn more at all. But still my awareness grew and became stronger and stronger. This was when I became aware of tarot and pendulums. I knew Divine God would speak messages to me via these tools, but still my father was strict and wary. I trusted in them. Somehow, I just knew they were psychic tools to guide, but I didn't get my own until many years later, when I would use them in readings to bring answers and guidance to others.

When I was 13, I had the opportunity to go on an adventure holiday to the south of France for ten days. I went with a few friends, filling a coach from Scotland with scouts, on their way through. On the second day of the trip a few slightly older boys introduced themselves. This was to be my first psychic acquaintance with real evil. One lad in particular sent chills running through me. I can still remember this vividly and it still sends chills through me even now when I notice this in others, true evil darkness. He was surrounded by black energy and darkness running through his being. He was what I can only describe as evil, or at least the forces of evil were working with him.

The holiday went well until the last night. The teachers gave everyone a free rein and we all hung out. As the evening developed, I noticed something was being planned, but kept away with my friends. Later in the evening we had gathered and some older lads had gotten hold of some alcohol. A small glass of wine was being passed around and I suddenly felt trapped. I was encouraged to try it, and I guess I just sealed my fate. Sure, enough the evil lad had spiked it with horse tranquillisers and I was led off. Before I could do anything, I collapsed, paralysed then they raped me.

I don't know how I made it home. But I survived. It was nothing short of Divine intervention. As horrific as the experience was, at the time I left my body. It was as though my spirit left, thankfully, not needing to be abused like my body. This is something I believe the Divine does to people under horrific circumstances, and I believe this happens to animals too. The Divine does not let us suffer what we can't manage. It was not my time to go. We must remember these things.

I got home and my family sat round the table for dinner. I was not in a good way inside and it showed.

At that point in time I had two huge choices, both would have massive yet very different consequences. I could tell my family, or not. My dad really made my mind up for me. He asked what was up and then quickly decided I had met a boyfriend and I was love sick. That was enough. I could not break his heart. So, I nodded, and then I forgot. It was at that point that the memory of the event miraculously disappeared, as it went it left me empty and full of no feelings. I did not recall the incident after that until six years later. My joy for life was gone in that instant, but it was to return.

It was that night that I lay on my bed feeling close to death. So close that I feared leaving life and my family. So strong was this feeling I could even see the image of a coffin around me. I said the only thing I knew, the Lord's Prayer, that was to be the start of an 18-year ordeal of challenge, trials and ill health and it started with a spirit visiting me. My grandfather who died years before I was born. He came to my bed as a light, I could see the shape of his nose and I recognised him from a photograph I had seen. Mostly I instinctively knew he was connected to my mum and yes indeed, he had the same shaped nose as her. I knew he was family and he confirmed it was grandad. He looked as though he had tears but he spoke to my heart. He told me 'What has happened is a terrible thing, you will not die, you will be very poorly for 18 years, but then you will live a long and happy life.' At first I thought, that's a life sentence, but his message was to get me through, and it did, it was a message of hope and I remembered it often.

I can only describe the next 18 years as my soul challenge. We all have a soul contract and our experiences are decided with us before we enter this life, as is our soul family whom we travel our lives with forever. I was shown a vision of this agreement. I was stood with my family in the spirit world and I clearly remember not wanting to return to life on earth. I was needed along with my soul family, we are a team, working with the Divine and there really is no choice in this. God had a purpose for me in good time. In my vision I remembered saying 'Ok I will go back but I want to experience the worst of life so that I never have to return again.' I remember the words mental illness, oppression and affliction. But I also remember that this time in my earth life would not be for it all and that I should experience a joyful life afterwards and enduring throughout my future to be. We all have a soul purpose or Divine purpose. This is our true calling and comes from the light in our soul. Sometimes people find this purpose early in life, perhaps they are born with an illness or disability and become a beacon of hope and light for others. Others may find it later perhaps after university or another form of study and they go on to teach, or be an inventor, bringing Divine inspiration to the world. To some it may be in the form of a hobby or charity work, kindness truly is the purest, brightest and indeed strongest display of the Divine Gods light. For me, as I was told it would come after my 18 years of challenge and ill health. In progressing into my current career as a spiritual practioner, I can bring all my experiences, apathy and understanding into my work alongside my spiritual abilities to help others and bring light and healing.

During this 18-year time, I was physically attacked twice and I had a miscarriage from the incident, even my home had an attempted arson attack. The worst in life and people, I had experienced it first hand and seen it all. But I never forgot the Divine God, love for myself, my family and my future and of course Divine God's promise through grandad. The devil is real, but a coward and has no control over those who despise him. It is up to us all to banish his hold and do and trust in the work of the Divine God and the comfort of Jesus.

To the time precisely, 18 years later, my ordeal was over, never to return. No more stays in mental health hospitals, having stayed 13 times, sometimes for up to eight months, and life started a wonderful, magical new beginning. Just as grandad had foretold. Now a wife and a mother of a beautiful daughter, I have developed my spiritual gift and learnt how to use my mediumship to bring peace, love, light, direction and clarity through to others. I mastered the skill of psychically and spiritually bringing messages through via the tarot as well as confidently bringing through loved ones. A great ability I have acquired over my years of study and meditation was spiritual philosophy, the knowledge reasoning and answers of life for me, which is the method I use in my readings. Like speaking from a place of knowledge whilst offering guidance or giving perspective on a vision I receive and explaining its meaning. Many times I have received the oracle card message,

'Share your wisdom'. In spiritual terms a grasp on spiritual philosophy is indeed wisdom. Which is not surprising though is necessary when helping others, as being a medium is open to all energies it makes perfect sense to endeavour to understand and gain knowledge on all spiritual aspects.

As a mother and housewife I was in a position to work from home and devote my full time to mastering my practice via study, daily meditation of up to two hours a day and general practise for me with my cards, pendulum and prayer intentions. In total my study took five years alongside regularly attending a spiritual development group. This is not to say my development stopped there though I left or as I prefer to say 'graduated' from the development circle – although open to all levels, I felt I had stopped learning there and knew it was time to fly the nest! I continue to read and practise spirituality every day in some form or another, after all I have always been a medium just now I have 'honed' my ability. On holiday for example I will look to my surroundings for inspiration, guidance or a message, having always gathered information via energy my whole life. A large part of my gift is service to Divine God. I know when I'm meant to pursue something by my relationship with God and the pull of his universal energy, being love. In my early business days I had just this feeling. I had a mission to spread the Divine God's message of love, care, hope and light across the world, and I set up a Facebook campaign, attracting over 10,000 followers worldwide on which I posted twice or three times a day, every day for three months until

I felt God's light, I was to share had achieved what it was meant to and it did. My true Divine mission had begun and God was to use my experiences and natural ability to reach across his world. I have sent healing intention and energy to war-torn countries and helped people spiritually and psychically whom I've never met, in another country. What non-mediumistic people struggle to understand is how indeed this could work? My answer is simple in a complex way! It is near impossible to explain what it is like to be a medium to someone who is not. It is a sixth sense or ability, but no more special than someone who is a great engineer. Yes it is different, but if you can imagine like in physics that everything and that means feelings, situations, thoughts and emotions are energy, then that is what I can decode. If I choose to give it my intention of course. It's wonderful and magical, but as I will explain later terrifying too. However fearful I have been, this too I was able to overcome and like us all I was able to master my fears by facing them. Knowledge is power hence my long time devoted to studying mediumship in all its facets and ways. I no longer fear.

Throughout the rest of this book, I wish to share with you all that Divine God has taught me, through my gift of being a medium, which opens my existence to many levels, secrets and magical mysteries. The Divine God is great and has blessed me with knowledge which never seizes to amaze, inspire and bring beauty to my life every day. This book is about my personal experience of mediumship. I get knowledge and answers from every subtle sense.

I see light and darkness in people and situations and through my meditations I travel to different realms of the spirit world visiting wonderful, amazing places meeting spirit beings and have visited mystical realms where dragons exist who work with the archangels against darkness and evil. I have been shown what the Divine does with evil souls and the place where they go outside of heaven. I have assisted a traumatised soul on its journey to the spirit world, I have worked to bring comfort with my spirit animal guide my pony, called Lisa. I have felt the terror of someone being murdered, tasting and smelling blood, though it happened down the town away from myself and I have visited my late father via meditation where he now lives in heaven in the spirit world.

There are many levels or realms in the spirit world and I believe some souls travel between them to work for and with Divine God and his archangels and ascended masters. I call these souls 'spiritual warriors'. But at 'home time' I believe the spirit realm they reside, to be called heaven to me. And it is exactly that a land of all your best thoughts, peaceful, happy, contented and with your loved ones. Before my father passed, we talked from the heart about spiritual things. I was able to give him comfort and told him of his freedom in the next life. Being a medium I knew I'd visit him in my meditations and I promised him and kept that promise. Before my father died, he told me he saw angels around him. This is not uncommon for anyone near passing. Most of all my father finally understood my ability and instead of his scepticism I felt like I finally had permission to share it and be honest about it with others, like finally 'coming out'. It is not easy to convince others of the things I'm aware of and see that others don't, nor is it appropriate to character analyse people in the supermarket or down the street, so I don't. My off switch is in fact by consciously choosing not to put my intention or awareness out there or to others, unless of course they have chosen to visit me for a reading. With being who I am comes a great level of trust and responsibility and in general I don't share it or talk about it at all, I'm just an everyday person. My relationship with Divine God is strong and powerful and what he has allowed me to experience, feel, sense and know has at times felt overwhelming. But we have an understanding, I would never want to not be a medium I wouldn't know what else to be to be honest. Just as many people would find being a medium strange, perhaps overwhelming, like wise I would find not being a medium strange and I would feel a lacking in some way I'm sure of it. God listens, I do fear God in the sense that I fully respect him, but he will always provide and show the way. Having comfort is different and is dependent on the times. At busy or difficult times, I work harder to bring Gods light through my everyday life, being receptable to whatever the vibes are, near and around the world. But the Divine God's promises never change. I have my promises and with that is always hope and trust.

However unbelievable my experiences as a medium may seem, it is however real. It is understandable as the human mind likes proof and if people are not a medium it is a case of opening their mind. Some do and some don't. Everyone can believe it if they choose to be open to spirituality and its wonders, wether we are open to spirituality or not, we are all of Gods light and our Divine God wants us all to stay in his light and be at peace inside and out. Not everyone is born a medium, nor do I believe it is something you can just choose to be one day. It is unique to the individual and it takes bravery, dedication and trust to understand how it works and it took years to learn how best I can share it with others. As with anything in life, in being a medium there are always new experiences and opportunities to evolve from, but I am a firm believer that you can master your gift in order for these new experiences to be most beneficial. In order to become a master of my own gift, I spent many years understanding my experiences both light and the dark side, learning from these experiences what I was prepared to work with and what not. There are many options as a medium such as psychic detective solving crime with the police, platform demonstrations of mediumship to name a couple but I felt most comfortable working one to one from home and sharing my gift through the written media. I spent a lot of hours studying spiritual concepts, through books and online sources and many hours in meditation or dream state, visiting my guides and learning about the spirit world.

I have guides that I work closely with which include ascended masters and more ethereal or mystical entities such as my dragon and what may be classed as my goddess or female who is of God.

They are comforting spirit forms, all from different higher realms and under the guidance and protection of the Divine God's archangels, Gods higher council and of course Jesus. I mention Jesus particularly because spirituality incorporates all faiths and I was shown a vision of the importance of Jesus' work in particularly with God. Jesus a medium himself is a master healer and has great power in bringing comfort and compassion. Although there are many prophets and important figures from every religion who work for God's council.

We have many earthbound lifetimes until the Divine God decides that our earth lessons are done. I have been told that me and my soul family are now on our final earthbound lifetime. We will then continue God's work via the spirit world, heaven. Having been shown a past life I was shown that I was a sister to my now mother and her partner was in fact my now father. It is the case that souls will have different roles in each other's lives but soul groups don't change and you will always be together, but likewise as with my parents, soul couples or twin flames remain together forever. It is important to remember this. We will never be without those we hold dearest, our loved ones, this is forever. Put together by reasons only the Divine God knows but still it is that way. It is important to remember that soul groups can and do involve friends too and we generally know this by the special connection we feel for them. All reassuring in this life when it gets hard or we feel alone, though we may have some lonely times these will never be long term and we are always connected ultimately.

I was told by my guide that I have always had this gift of psychic mediumship in effect it is just who I am. Now I wish to share this and what I have learnt with you. Though I appreciate much will seem far out I hope it will open your mind allowing God's light to enter bringing healing, guidance and inspiration to your life, in your own unique way. We all have it within us to make a difference and make the world on which we live a better place, but we can't achieve the Divine God's full vision of a heaven on earth without the direction and assistance of spirit. Within us all, we can all try our best to be open to this vision and do our own bit, whatever that is to the individual. My father was a great man and had hundreds of people attend his funeral. In his own words written before he died and read out that day to all was, 'Make the world a better place.' We all have talent and or gifts that each individual can capitalise on, reaching their full potential is what changes the world, person by person, whatever the gift. Besides difference is good and indeed what makes the world work.

Energies

Being a medium energy is a very big part of my daily life. Having a so called sixth sense an energy radar detects even the subtlest energy. Energy makes up everything and it's what tells me everything. It is almost another language and I believe it is this ability which can be termed as a sixth sense. Energy is in nature, and in and around people. Energy makes up situations, I can read this and it is the basis of my spiritual readings. Energy is also how spirits communicate, transferring knowledge, visions, smells and sensations. As everything is made of energy it is far too complex to break it down and analyse everything as a medium, I have learnt to switch on and off this ability or sixth sense as to get along with my own day. However, I don't believe I ever turn it off completely, I don't think I can but I decide when 'I'm working' and when I'm not. For example, in terms of percentage if I was doing a full spiritual reading, I would be 100% switched on. On holiday for example I'd just bubble along at 10%. If I was around difficult people or a difficult situation I would likely be 30% in order to gauge the best outcome, but on a usual basis out and about I would not aim to be switched on as on holiday, as it is neither any of my business nor a suitable use of my ability to read anyone and everyone, so unless someone has asked for a reading, no I don't, besides it would be easy to discover things you wish you hadn't known.

Energy is everything, it is easy for me as a medium to tell you this as I sense first, for example rather than see or smell. I get feelings and process those feelings into information. Trees for example as we all know are living things but they have energy and can hold messages if I were to tune in. After all they have been around a very long time and hold great wisdom if you are akin to sensing what they have to tell you. The cycles of the moon have a huge impact on the energy of that month. As in astrology the different planets hold energy which affects our solar system and their different alignments bring the world different shifts in energy. Of course we need to embrace these changes, the Divine God wants us to reap the rewards and be both happy and successful in life. It was a great breakthrough when I spent time to understand moon cycles, each different, however being in tune with what they have to offer and setting my prayers to the Divine God and my intentions within my own life at the time of a waxing and full moon made me feel so much more in the flow of the universal energy as a whole. Again, I already sensed these shifts in energy though up until recently I hadn't seeked to understand it so I felt pushed along rather than being in the flow. One of my biggest problems I had to overcome was rushing forward, my late Grandpa had told me to 'Slow down or you'll miss the beauty.' I believe this rushing was a bad habit picked up from my traumatic years, when indeed I needed that fight and determination to push through, perhaps so much I struggled to switch it off although I no longer needed it.

Of course, on Earth unfortunately evil energies still exist. I say still exist because I do believe along with many other spiritually minded people I have spoken to, that currently we as a world are in a stage of spiritual evolution and obviously the Divine God's ultimate purpose being a state of heaven on earth. However, evil does still try and some do follow it. People under the influence of this darker energy will often give most people a sense of uneasiness, as a medium being open to this is not a nice experience. There was a short time in my development where I walked around completely aware of the darker energies around. It was as if the Divine was showing me, likely in order to help my readings, and for my own learning and development purposes. Unfortunately, during this short time, I had a disturbing night's sleep whilst on holiday. I woke with great terror and I could taste and smell blood, it lasted a while then I heard spirit say 'dead' then it went away. I was attending a spiritual church group at the time and I asked my tutor what it meant, she said I had picked up on something and that I should look into the news the around the time. I did and it turned out that there had in fact been a murder down in the town. Now I understand that this is not a regular occurrence but it certainly showed me what as a medium I can detect. At this point I would rather not know about these types of things but what it taught me was to honour my ability and make suitable decisions with my guides as to what and when I want the worlds evil to experience. Of course, I was perfectly safe and nowhere near the incident really and there are mediums who thrive off this type of mediumship, working with the police and CIA.

It is not for me, I'm thankful for the experience of finding out that this is not for me and it enabled me to set boundaries for myself and with spirit. This was probably my biggest learning curve; it was not comfortable but hey it's real too. With the Divine and Jesus there is nothing to fear but it seems there are times that the devil gets his way but darkness is always the lesser power and over everything The Divine God's ultimate will is done. We will all pass from this life one way or another we must find our own peace with how as in our predestined soul contract for life on earth this experience as with all transitions have already been decided with us for the development of our soul's journey, before we entered this life.

Angels

When I was a young child, there was so much joy around my family, the friends we shared with and the wonderful farm we lived on. My first awesome experience with an Archangel was on our back lawn, a beautiful old house and the back lawn was known as the tennis court, as it had often been used as. There was a grand tree at the bottom end. We had been with friends, there were many people about, something to do with the farm. I remember playing joyfully on the tennis court when my attention was drawn to this awesome bright light over the oak tree. It was almost like a portal to heaven had opened and there in the light was a massive figure of an angel. When I say massive, Archangels are not human-sized they really are ginormous. I believe I was the only one who saw it. I remember there being an upwards funnel from the Archangel to highest heaven. I could see many other angels higher up. It felt like the true love of Divine God and Jesus' love, that powerful type of love. I don't remember how it was dressed just that it was a truly dazzling bright, bright, white light. I felt quite dumbfounded. All I can remember afterwards is my mother scooping me up and taking me in for a nap. The only other times I've seen Archangels was in my bedroom where I now live, still on the farm in the farm cottage. This Archangel I know was one of inspiration she was Indian looking and wore an ornate sash. She was also very tall and filled the room to the high roof, she came to me at a time when I was recovering from an illness and I was searching for inspiration in my life. I remember seeing another Archangel I believe he was Archangel Michael and he offers us strength especially at times when we need to cut our ties with the past, at times of transition and moving on. He visited me as I was leaving my 18 years of illness and challenges behind me. We can all call on his help through a small prayer in our minds at these sometimes-tricky times in our lives. He too was very tall, masculine in appearance and carried a sword. Though he didn't show me the sword but he told me it was there. Archangels are different to spirit family. When spirit loved ones present them self, they look just like the human form of that person and wear the clothes that the person would have chosen to wear in life. The most wonderful and fascinating time for earth and angels is on the weeks running up to Christmas. At this time of year, the Divine God sends special Christmas angels to touch each and every one of us with Divine light. They will also be reminding us to look out for symbols of love and are often the reason behind our charity at this time of year, silently dropping us God Divine's miraculous light of love into our hearts, minds and souls. This is where I believe the term Christmas spirit comes from, don't we all feel that extra love and sparkle at Christmas? Wonderful, just beautiful.

One fascinating experience I remember was the day after a lad died, I had seen him only a week before. I was shocked at his death and I remember sitting on my spare bed and feeling sorry about it. Just then I saw a white misty substance floating in front of me, I now know this is called ectoplasm. As I marvelled at it suddenly a fully formed in colour figure of this lad stood. In his jeans and t-shirt I felt I had to say something so I said how sorry about things I was, then he left. This type of mediumship is rare I have never seen it happen since it is known as physical mediumship. Though I had not asked it to happen, it just did, physical mediumship was practised more so in Victorian times and has never been practised in any group I've been in. However I regularly catch glimpses of human-size light in places, to me it's very natural to share the world with spirit. They are spirits just travelling and sharing , doing their own thing, not always wanting to communicate. As a medium, i can see through the veil to the spirit world. It is also like having a lightbulb over your head, to the spirit world. Spirits are attracted to mediums because we are people who can detect their energy and can pass messages on their behalf and speak with them. But likewise, I can ask spirit to leave and they will. At one time it was very overwhelming and would make me agitated and it was not sustainable. Now I have learnt how to decide not only with my guides but with spirit in general, that there is a suitable time and place for conversing with them, as in when someone comes for a reading, otherwise I have nothing to offer them and don't require anything from them. It has become a relaxed and mature approach. In affect, it's always been this way for me, I've grown up with it. I've been overwhelmed by spirit linked to my bouts of mental illness as you might imagine. Being a medium has given me nothing short of hell, by means of overwhelming, societies lack of acceptance, my loved ones bewilderment, but in any and all of the negatives being a medium of energy, love, has got me through, offering me comfort, messages and escapism and left me appreciating the beauty of life and people. It is important to remember to be polite to spirits, however, as they were people once and their personalities remain the same as on earth. Forceful and with authority, however, when moving unwanted spirits on. It can be very exciting and is an honour to see them when so many people don't, after all.

Healing

In being born a medium and open to energies of all and any kind it seemed natural that with my nature of wanting to help animals, nature and people that I would channel this energy to heal. From a young age I was aware of this ability where healing energy can transfer via touch and intention allowing God's healing to occur. I found that animals would trust me quickly with this same gentle energy. Archangel Raphael works with healing and the colour green means healing to me. If something needs healing, I concentrate on the colour green and other colours too like pink for comfort and of course the white and violet light of the Divine God. I have seen pain disappear quickly and certain knocks and injuries heal quickly and effectively. Once I helped my Dad save a prize calf by focusing this healing energy by rubbing the ends of its ears which are sensitive points.

I was diagnosed with an illness and had many stays in hospital spanning a period of 18 years. Though I was ill, I never truly felt like I was suffering in that time apart from odd times but if I ever did feel like I was suffering it never lasted long and it would pass. I always knew it would pass too. In the same way that energy can heal physically it can heal emotions and lift spirits too. The energy of Love is most powerful and a marvellous thing. And it is a mind which directs this flow of energy, good or indeed bad.

A medium is essentially a medium of energy. When energy passes to me, I can determine information from it, or not if I switch off, but nevertheless this ability has taught me a great deal. Like the five senses of sight, sound, smell, taste and touch, being a medium of energy is indeed as a sixth sense. Just as we gather information from our senses I gather information from energies which I sense from people objects and situations, and this is how I can help people with complex problems whom I've never even met, just being seeing a photo of them or is how I read tarot cards, once the client has transferred their energy via shuffling the cards. I decode the information through pictures and symbols in my mind's eye, a knowing and occasionally I can hear a word or two, usually in my mind like I get a name and I think that wasn't me! For example, a lady came to me and after connecting with her via the tarot cards that she had shuffled and with her late relative whom was in spirit that we had contacted, I was shown her house and able to describe it in great detail. Spirit energy will often show you around houses pointing out things of importance and always showing you a pet too if they had one. All of these things are evidence to the client who has chosen to visit myself as a medium of energies between the spirit world and earth and indeed the horizontal energies of time. The idea that one can see into the past and the future is to do with energy and a trained medium can tune in ahead of the here and now or before on what are known as the Akashic records, the idea that pathways of life are of somewhat a predestined entity. Of course, it is known there are more than one pathway we can choose from. It is thought seven. Once on a chosen pathway as a medium I can follow that particular pathway forward for example but through tarot either the outcome of that particular pathway or other pathways may show up as better. Either way that is where my counsel comes in, though it is always the choice of the client to decide what they choose and I always work with the upmost discretion, I am only the messenger.

It is an honour, a privilege and my true purpose to work with my gift or ability as a medium. It is not something I rushed into by any means, in fact I tried nursing and community outreach office work at first. Though it kept hitting me harder the more I choose to pursue other career paths. I guess I doubted how it would work out and setting up my own business meant there was no known outcomes. Again, trusting in higher powers and going with the flow remains my best option, happiest option and ultimately my most successful. It is known in the spiritual world that one's greatest successes come from following a passion, as passions are just exaggerated feelings of the soul's truest path and purpose.

The Power of Thought

As everything is essentially a form of energy, rock for example denser than wind, but even rock has a vibrational frequency that, if attuned to, a medium like myself could pick up on. Crystals are a good example of rock or stone which hold unique energy depending on where they are from and how they are formed. A rose quartz holds a very loving and healing energy whereas a clear quartz rids negativity. Crystal healing is a popular therapy, but anyone can benefit from a crystal especially ones you are drawn too.

Just as crystal energy has known meanings, the energy of people and places do too. If we imagine that everything is energy and that we in our minds as thoughts are the controller, then just like switching over a TV channel, we too can think where and what we need to do, become or change. The same with bad situations and challenges. We can determine if we see it either positively or negatively and make choices on how to move on.

With negative emotions too, we can choose to dwell or to put it behind us. We all have this ability. So much stress in people's lives is because they have failed to pick up the controller and metaphorically speaking change channels. A good process for putting this into practice is to as soon as you wake up be thankful for nature and the new day then decide what you need to do today and then pick up the controller and select how you wish to approach it, what attitude will you choose to approach the challenges of your day? Will it be hard work and determined or with a sense of fun? Then go get it! There is far more talk and on social media about our thoughts being positive etc, now more than ever, and it is so important. If you could choose to suffer or to be relaxed and thankful, you would surely choose to be relaxed and thankful, but too many people don't realise that it is up to them to choose. Often the miracles are activated from within our very selves and all it takes is an opposite thought process to activate a better outcome and there is your miracle. Miracles for humans are on the smallest scale a release or shift of circumstances activated by thought and action. In combined energies of a shift in thought and action, whereby whole communities, countries or even the world comes together, just think of the scale of the miracles! So many people just wait for the miracle to happen, what spirit has told me is that we as the light of God have to put these thoughts and changes into action and into the world ourselves and in fact be the facilitator of manifesting our miracles.

Soul Groups

I find soul groups fascinating and very comforting. As a medium I have been shown certain things about what soul groups are and how they work. There are a few things that I have learnt mainly about my own soul group but a bit about other soul groups too. Firstly, I know that soul groups always stay together, over many lives and in the spirit world. That is how our loved ones can be contacted, often coming through as a group of people family and or friends. We all have some special connections in life most obviously our immediate family. We feel great love for them and a sense of belonging and contentment with them. I was shown a previous life where my parents were part of and I have also been shown a future in the spirit world where all my close family as I know them are at a gathering or party. These visions are real and are part of my ability to see psychically, into what are known as the Akashic records. The record of events and any given time past or future. They are there for all but personalised to the individual.

We talk about friends coming and going and sometimes even the breakdown of family. We can ask many questions about why. Sometimes it is ourselves who feel forced to make the choice to break away from the negativity or drama of others. But this can leave us lost and confused. It is not uncommon for a close relationship break down to feel like grief and loss. Often people come into our lives only for a short time to help our soul grow, then we move on. Sometimes someone will be in our life for a reason and a time. When this ends this separation is usually well understood and accepted. More occasionally separation is where by two souls agree to grow together but then one of the people gets comfortable, not wanting to progress whilst the other continues to grow. This particular circumstance is a personal choice and the one wanting to continue on the path of progression should not feel bad although most likely will feel sad. When a soul actively chooses not to progress in this life, the lessons will still need to be learnt. We are usually born into our soul group, with some exceptions and sometimes soul members will join our lives at a later time. Whenever they are there you can recognise them by being the close connections that are always there and that stick around. This is also the case for our beloved pets, they too form lasting connections with us and will remain in our soul's journey forever. I have been shown that when animals pass they are granted their spiritual right to freedom, they are still connected to their human loved ones and will spend time with them, if they are in heaven too. If the person is on earth it is also common for the spirit pet to visit their beloved owner and friend. In spirit or heaven, they are free to explore, have adventures and play, joining with other animals.

Visions, Knowing and Dreams

When I talk about visions some are in my mind's eye and some visions are a knowing, different from encounters with angels or spirit visions they often take me to the spirit world, or project me into the Akashic records of the future. One thing I believe about what I call visions is that they always project a better and positive scenario, showing the light. It is different from the knowing of a bad thing about to happen. Visions show hope and a way forward. They don't always show something that will happen exactly in that way but they always leave me feeling wiser, more prepared and positive. I have the ability to imagine a future situation and see it as it could play out. I don't do this apart from in a reading because it is not helpful to live in the future and can be quite difficult and stressful to chop and change. Also, it is always best to live in the here and now to gain the most from every experience and to remain balanced and happiest.

Always if I'm meant to know and pass on something to someone, I will always be shown it and through my development I learnt to just trust, it will come in when it's meant to, so I can remain switched off, unless in a reading. These types of visions are most common and easy to manage, it gives light to what it fully means to be a medium in society and it is not just to give someone a reading, it is an everyday way of life and proves that how a medium works is useful and helpful to others and society in general everyday life. In fact, I don't remember a day that it has not happened at all. It could be as little as a strong or bad feeling when walking past someone or noticing a spirit in a room of people. I usually get short snippets of information that are usually very helpful or useful to someone, a quick snapshot or prior knowing, it can relieve uncertainty, often these short visions or knowing's bring others reassurance and clarity and often when said to them it brings peace and a certainty. I would not prior announce that I am a medium or that I was about to pass on some vision. I learnt that as it is who I am and how I work as an individual I grew more confident as I got older to just say what I know or am shown as part of usual conversation. Like it is my opinion as worthy as anyone else's, when actually feeling like its coming from somewhere else. This was quite a tricky thing and it took me a really long time to be comfortable with the way I am as a medium and confident enough to do this effectively in my everyday life.

A medium is a vessel in simple form, when I accepted that is the way I have to work or be, it was a great breakthrough in my self-esteem and confidence with others, also with life. Being a medium I am meant to help others and my gift is not just for my own benefit. After all, not everyone is a medium and it is special to me. In affect it's like being an open line of communication to spirit and universal energies. The Divine God being at the very end of the line as the controller. This is particularly useful in times where there are difficult people or circumstances and really it is just bringing the truth to light which like it or not will always solve a problem one way or the other. It means I live with a great sense of justice.

I don't fear the devil's ways; I know I will be given the power to cope with anything and this has been the case with some of my soul challenges. Not everyone likes to hear the truth and more often people who I spent a lot of time with say in a group, will not like this energy around me and it makes them feel uncomfortable with their own self or chosen behaviour. I guess I bring to light without saying things, acting like a mirror for them, but in fact the energy they pick up is that of truth and justice, as a vessel of the Divine God's light, it couldn't be anything else. Just because as a medium I am a vessel for this and greater good by the nature of my energy. This displeases some and I have known on more than one occasion friends abandon me in order to pursue a lifestyle less savoury. Not that I pass verbal judgement but It is not my purpose to resonate with negative behaviours. I have learnt not to speak out, stress this fact or argue, even I've learnt not to hold on and just keep moving to the next thing. Most of all I've learnt it is out of my control. I am a medium and a vessel of the light, and in blunt terms the devil will not like it. Any bad choices boiled down will, whether people accept or not, be influenced by evil or darker energy which filters into people making a bad choice look good if you like. The people who fall for it will be the ones who don't grow in the light but remain stuck in negative behaviours. Being a medium, challenges this by my very nature, and some people choose not to like or take notice of themselves. I say take notice of themselves because one thing my job as a medium is not to preach or tell others what to think, but bring light, through the vessel I am as medium, which is to help them to help themselves. After all we can indeed only see our flaws and make changes to help ourselves ultimately. In other words, in a less than savoury friend group, act like a mirror to others, forcing them to make a decision on their behaviours and choices one way or another. This is not my problem, I am what I am if I have to move away and onwards I will.

Shamanic Influence

Having a keen interest in nature and experiencing the energy of nature and animals as a medium and picking up on the language of nature too I was drawn to study the shamanic influences of a medium. Shamans originate in indigenous cultures and are wise people who channel spirit, bring forth visions and healing, very similar to the way I experience being a medium. Shamans use plants and the sound vibrations of drumming to connect with spirit and to bring healing. Their pure connection to nature and spirit unaffected by the modern world intrigued and fascinated me. It seemed quite blissful to have medium abilities in such a seemingly simple environment, being able to be so pure with it seemed so much more uncomplicated than myself in the modern world environment, where different work routines among other routines, finances etc. are all so prevalent. What the shamanic way has taught me was how I could incorporate this calm mediumship into my way of life. I began religiously meditating for up to two hours every single day for well over a year. During these mediations I learnt a shamanic technique called journeying. This was an advancement in my mediumship and it took me to a new level of working. Not just day to day visions and knowing but actual journeying into the spirit world. In the spirit world I met my spirit animal guide my old pony called Lisa, my oldest best friend, and we travelled together through beautiful landscapes, through forest and past magical healing pools with waterfalls. Often Lisa and I would stop to swim and play in the water and I would experience its healing properties. This is also where I met the Ascended Master called Master Michael. We always travelled the same way whenever we met Master Michael it was over a bridge to a cave where we could find him. At first, I thought he lived there but I later learnt that this was where he worked from and he would return to his family and people. But whenever since I have met Master Michael it is always at this same cave. Master Michael is a spiritually gifted, powerful man and once he would have spent life on earth. He is now an ascended master which is of a higher spiritual power than spirit people but below the archangels, who in turn are under the Divine God himself and Jesus and his council. Like a hierarchy of spiritual powers. Among the realms of Archangels also dragons exist they work alongside archangels to banish evil. Dragons are gracious comforting powerful creatures of God. In one of my journeys I met one.

Master Michael was a great source of inspiration and help in my worldwide spiritual campaign on Facebook. Master Michael works with energy but in a highly skilled and powerful way, very refined. In his cave he had a stone mixing pot which was the sacred place for very powerful magic to occur. I think saying spells has negative connotations and links to evil witches, though spells are most powerful when used under the power of God and Christ's white violet light for good. Good energy is more powerful than evil energy and can banish evil and also provide protection against evil energy. An Ascended Master is God's worker of great magic, power and importance. Master Michael gave me the sparkle that drove my campaign. In the time when I visited him often, I was very active in my spiritual development. In fact, I was so immersed it was quite intense. Master Michael offered advice and reassurance and gave me courage. I guess I was graduating like the final exams. In spiritual terms it is called initiation but not into a group initiation, of yourself, initiation as a working medium intense and took a lot of study and application. It would not be good to remain in that state all the time I would say it lasted a few months within that whole number of years developing. But like everything it came to an end. It was then that I was fully able to enjoy ordinary life but open up to work competently with spirit for a reading. I attended a lot of spiritual groups but after this time of initiation I felt I only really wanted to work when someone asked for a reading, and in the meantime enjoy ordinary life. In total this whole full circle of commitment to mediumship took five years and I was left able to control my gift and use it beneficially for others in readings. With my disrupted educational years due to many bouts of illness and hospital stays, I felt short-changed in regard to a career for a time. I started a nursing course but again had to leave with ill health. Eventually the thing that was always there after me trying various jobs was my spiritual gift and actually because of my ill health it opened up the opportunity to pursue spirituality in great detail and from home. It was meant to be.

Looking back, it was the largest commitment I've made to a project or career option, including nursing.

I was successful at singing, including being in a band and getting recognised by a London label. I loved pursuing them both. But God had other long-term plans and when he deemed me ready was when my full-time commitment and journey of mediumship began. It was a calling and all in God's Divine timing. Every day for five years a combination of study, meditation, and practice. When I look back, I do think wow! That was full going and then I'm happy that I've ended up doing what comes most naturally, helping others, being useful with my gift and living a peaceful, fulfilling life writing to share with others. I would never want to live my life again my past although at the time I coped well, looking back fills me with dread. It was very hard, very scary and very demanding of a great deal of faith.

The Spirit World

There are four realms that I have been shown, there are three below, Earth being one, but I've never been shown the two lower spirit realms. In the order I was shown: the first being heaven, then the realm of Archangels and Ascended masters, then the mystical realm where dragons exist then god's council the highest. Archangels and ascended masters can go between realms as can any spirit being whom I call spiritual warriors. I do like to reiterate that heaven is like home and travelling as a spirit or any other entity would be like going to work. But doing God's work. The ultimate purpose of the irradiation of all evil and certainly assisting this upon earth.

Going back to God's purpose and looking back at my life thus far although I'm far from elderly I know that my life's journey is of three parts. The first my idyllic childhood, the second the 18-year ordeal of illness and challenges, leading to the final part being my life as an enduring medium. I guess I would not have felt able at all to one, do readings, and two, write and share this message if I hadn't had the idyllic start which set me on good footing, followed by the gritty dark life experience which is of course reality too. Darkness is always a choice by someone in the first instance. If everyone took control not to follow the devil's ways there would be no darkness as there would be no use for the devil and his energy would be irradiated. The devil feeds of people who do his work and like a leech will try to attach itself to others along the way. With simple disregard, no one has to follow.

It is always our choice. Without humans who follow, the power that evil has, would be non-existent. It is humans who choose evil who feed its power. I, however as my soul contract was decided, was willing to be a victim of the devil's darkness through others. I agreed to experience this as part of my soul contract in order for it to subsequently lead me to a better life and one with true empathy, it is not uncommon for people in their soul contract to choose to be a victim at some point in their life, in order to grow. Of course, these experiences have helped me when doing readings for people who indeed themselves come from all walks of life and experiences. This leads me to say that being a medium on earth is by no means easy. To fully recognise the use for me that God has planned I really had to make sacrifices in this life, agreed not for it all, but for 18 years. God has never left me though I may have wondered at one time, just one last push to the finish line. I'm not going to lie, I was angry at God at one point but my anger didn't serve me but still I know God understood. When I one day found myself out of this 18-year period, to be honest I didn't really know how to trust in life and enjoy it at first. It took time to find my new feet and embrace a peaceful future at last. Although I moved into a much better part of my life it was not easy to transition from the one extreme to the other. I was grateful as ever to the calming, stable influence of my family. But I'm independent always have been. I don't rely on a group of others for my happiness or indeed for anything including my experiences. Everyone is a friend if they are kind and nice if you like. Of course,

I see more of certain people and make arrangements to do things as and when such circumstances arise. But no one can live your life for you and I have seen others fall into the trap where they rely on their friend so much that neither of them truly achieves goals and development. Knowing the outcome of such behaviour as a medium I was shown that that a lack of self-progress now doesn't mean that it gets skipped out, you will have to address this personal evolution either in this life sooner or later or indeed the next life. Most of us will automatically follow our soul contract, it's the inner drive that pushes us to pursue and achieve things and we follow it to our best abilities. That is all that the Divine God expects of us and by following it we in return can expect God's love and protection and of course the angel's assistance and indeed our place in heaven. For those who choose not to follow the path of their soul contract have been led astray somehow, unfortunately this is nothing short of the devil's plan. The devil is against anything of God so in affect he is winning if people are turning away from their soul contract with God. These people are only punishing themselves by not taking action to get back on the right path or by falling for the temptations of this perhaps seemingly easier, more appealing in some way, lifestyle. Maybe it was chosen out of hardship or difficulties, where the devil's way found a weakness and persuaded them to this alternative life. However, even if this is the case it is always a choice and the right way will always be an evident option. I have seen this happen to someone I cared about. It is both sad and unnerving how the devil's ways creep into a person's self and life. It is quite obvious to me as a medium to be able to tell who is and who isn't on their right path. I get a knowing and it is recognisable by someone's demeanour. Someone on their true path will always appear lighter, come across friendlier and appear open as if nothing to hide. These people will be honest and will not be interested in nasty remarks. If someone has chosen a different path than that of their soul contract or right path, they will in simple terms not be any of the above and will come across more nastily. These people are less likely to be honest or trustworthy. It is never too late to get back onto the right path but I guess it's like heading 60 miles or so the wrong way down the motorway only to be pretty much back where you started. I'm not saying it's easy to know which choices because life on Earth as an experience is not easy. But knowing right from wrong and good from bad is the bottom line and in order to get on the wrong path at some point for whatever reason someone will have chosen a wrong or a bad. It is likely they will be aware of this themselves because it is the light of God within us that would tell us, whether someone listens to it is entirely up to them and they must face the consequences. Being on the wrong path is hazardous and attracts negativity in its essence. Hopefully people don't travel for 200 or more miles down the wrong way, metaphorically speaking, as it's likely that the longer you're on it the more problems that arise. This is not to say that someone on the right path will not have problems. More that the problems are part of their development which God would have fully equipped you for and of course support you through safely. Turning away from God is like not having a comfortable safety net. The types of consequences on the wrong path would appear worse or be more severe in effect than if the same situation was part of someone's soul journey.

Heaven and Hell

It intrigued me as a spiritual person, knowing the forces of evil and being victim to evil deeds, what the Divine God really did with these dark people. One day God showed me a vision. It was of a very small place outside of and just below heaven. Remember the spirit world is infinite, this place was small like an island. I was shown through vision and knowing that this place was certain evil souls' final destination, a place they don't return from and cease to exist as soul beings. This place I was told was for truly evil souls who have broken every contract with the Divine God, committed great atrocities and failed to follow the learning and growth of their true soul path. In effect they have even broken their own soul contract. The soul is taken. Instead of to a welcome home party with loved ones in heaven, it is taken by special spiritual warriors who work under the direction of the ascended masters and God's council, to this place, the dark soul does not enter heaven. I was shown that God himself extinguishes the soul, dissolves it with his pure light and it ceases to exist. This place is so small in comparison to the vastness of the spirit world which is reassuring as this is God's last resort for people who truly have done terrible things.

It intrigues and fascinates me as a medium to have been given this knowledge and understanding of the spiritual world and society and how it works. We as a world are in a time of great spiritual evolution. Now more than ever and of course through social media and TV, spiritually conscious people are sharing their words of knowledge and encouragement. Everyone is in essence spiritual and of Divine God or the light and millions of people are realising their purpose on earth whether it be to help animals or create the next environment-saving device. People are talking about it and sharing about it and there is a buzz around the ideology of a heaven on earth, God's ultimate plan if you like or as most people say a better world. More people are attending spiritual development groups learning and sharing from each other and more people are offering alternative therapies which include readings from mediums. Me pursuing being a medium fully is no different to the guy the same age working on environmentally friendly packaging from his office in a city. We all have a purpose and we can all make a difference to make the world a better place if we stay true to our soul contract, or the right path. You might say well how do I know if I am. My answer is you will know if you've chosen something wrong or bad in your life. Did you put it right? Do you have a positive goal in mind, something that would benefit humanity and the world in some way? If yes then you are likely on the right path, if you have no positive life affirming goals and you feel a sense of guilt about something it could be that you are not on your ideal path. If you still don't know a medium or shaman could help you. Commonly people will go through spiritual awakening, usually this time involves a lot of questioning and change. Change in ideals and goals. It is a process which at the other side of people end by living in their higher self, sharing their unique light. This state of being is what I have been shown is the earth as in heaven state. For some the transition is more subtle and gradual, for others it comes after trauma or some incident, however you get there you will be glad when you do. It is a state to celebrate in you and be thankful for all the beauty of earth and life. To be proud of yourself and accepting of life and death. In this time of transition, it is easy to feel overwhelmed and confused also fearful. My best advice to this is twofold. Firstly don't underestimate the devils attempts to throw you of your course, fear is a big way his influences creep in. However, it is important to realise this and that we have the power over our feelings, even as a receptive medium, we can still ask our guides to take impressions away and to agree the times we are working. As far as our own fears are concerned the best thing is to remember that we have a soul purpose and a predetermined soul contract that we are following and that the Divine God and his angels will be honouring, guarding, assisting and protecting that to ensure it happens. All we need do is follow our passions, goals, and dreams and trust, or as some may say follow our gut.

Around the time that I was called to begin my true spiritual work and service in 2015 and along my journey of being able to utilise my ability to help others, I had the most awesome experience. One night early evening I remember being in my kitchen. I went and picked up my phone and there was a picture of a guy laid at the bottom of some cliff face in a mountainous region. Weirdly I knew he had fallen and was injured and needed assistance though he was alone, all but his phone. I got the impression that he was dazed and that he couldn't move. He had a bright yellow coat on. I don't know how he got through to me apart from being a miracle but I knew I had to do all I could to help him. So, I contacted mountain rescue via Siri on my iPhone I couldn't tell if it would work, I just had this image which had taken over my phone screen, but I instinctively knew it was North England region and I was able to describe in detail what I had come up on my phone screen, indeed an image of him and where he had fallen. Then I waited. Sure, enough in a couple of days when I checked that local mountain rescue website, a man fitting my description and the area, had been found whilst hiking and had indeed fallen down the cliff. I knew it was him that was saved. God's miracles never seize to amaze me and often spirit use the internet and phone lines, as they do electrics and it is common for lights to flicker in a room where spirit is present. Spirit can manipulate these forms of energy transfer.

After this was another new stage and when my interest in bad people began, Interest in the sense of justice. I found that via Google maps real time where by the image of somewhere is actual, I could pick up on energies of people in cars who were criminals. It's like I knew spots where druggies would park up and that sort of crime. To be honest it is something some mediums will work with but it wasn't my calling long term so it came and went. I don't do it now. It does intrigue me and it is important work but I know it's not for me working with criminals and the police. My work is on a different level to assist people who are trying hard to reach their highest self on their path of enlightenment but have stumbling blocks. My work involves people who need some guidance and a little help, but deep down they are set on their true path, they are just struggling for one or many reasons. In a nutshell, my ability works with guidance, not punishment. That is a different kettle of fish which I've been told by my guides is not my work. But as in all good forms of study we learn about all aspects of a subject before we graduate.

Psychic detective

Psychic detective work is another world, I learnt about it through my own experience of it but it takes a special type of medium to work in that field long term. It involves firstly detection then assisting soul progression and in some extreme cases soul termination. It is by no means for the fainthearted and in my study years I did a short time in this type of medium role. Baptism of fire so to speak and it was during this time that I experienced a soul termination following a horrific murder, amongst many crimes. A soul termination is only for the way extreme people. They will, apart from living a generally bad way of life will have committed unspeakable crime. Unfortunately for them, there is a place for them and spirit deal with this, I have been shown in a dream. There is never any escaping the truth of love and God has workers for these consequences. Basically, the soul is taken to what I deem hell. Though not a hell pit of fire. A small place below heaven where souls are no less than extinguished by God Divine's light Himself, dissolved to nonexistence. A soul so dark and fruitless that the force of gods light disperses it from all eternity. An ascended master or guide in the spirit world will meet the soul and take it to this place of desolation. It is all controlled by God Divine's workers and God has told me that it is by no means an easy quick fix and that it is necessary, but thankfully quite rare in the scheme of things. Of course, God creates us to enjoy goodness and beauty, but those who turn away from him will be punished. When we have been seriously wronged or we know of someone who has by means of another person, just remember, there are consequences for everything. If it's not a lesson learnt then it's likely a dimmer outlook for them. Nothing is unseen. There will be a consequence.

Although I'm not meant to work with criminology it still intrigues me greatly. As a medium I already have a great sense of courage and although scary as a horror film, it does give me a great satisfaction, bringing justice to the worst of human form. I must let it go however as I have a different higher purpose and no way can I live between working both.

My understanding of the Divine God is that first and foremost he is everything positive we could ever have or hope to wish for, the beauty of Mother Earth, our successes and joys. But he like us, made in his likeness, God is not a pushover and not to be taken for granted. God is love, the energy that makes all creation. God is the only entity that has the power to override love in all its greatest forms. What I mean is consequences. We are not in control of this only God will direct. He wants us to be our best self. He knows each and every one of us intimately, like a class teacher. He wants us to succeed. We all can. If we choose. He gives us choice. But as a true father he will punish that which he deems unacceptable.

Spiritual Enlightenment, Also Known as Awakening to Higher Self

Spiritual enlightenment can be gradual or more sudden. Usually it is gradual, occasionally it occurs post trauma or a near-death experience, where you wake finding yourself somehow different. It is a heaven on earth but we're still on earth with others of different mindset. It doesn't matter you will always be happy inside when you reach your highest level of self. This is self being prepared for a great future in heaven where you will continue your work with those whom you are closely connected to, by soul family or by soul purpose.

Those who don't reach spiritual enlightenment or living through their highest self will have not have completed their soul lessons. It is not a given time thing but a choice. Choosing the wrong path in affect bad things or avoidance of true progress will take longer than say someone whose fought the good fight and always remained true to themselves above everything around them. Getting there will never be easy but it will I assure you be worth it. And in time you will begin to give back from a higher perspective by simply being you. Whatever family, friends and work interests you have.

Spiritual enlightenment is a state where you have little questions and little fears, in becoming fully aware of yourself as a soul you will have done soul searching and answered to your own darker side and in doing so made peace with your soul and self, living via your own truth inclines you to the truth of God and you begin to relax with your life and journey trusting and knowing that it is for your highest good. In the current time and the spiritual evolution that is upon us now, many, many people are finding their true selves and are awakening to this way of life living through their highest selves and bringing positive change to others and the world. However, there will be many who don't choose. Just as the world has striven for equality in all areas and aspects of life, so are we all equal to choose to live through our highest self. It is the small choices that determine our next step of progress holistically. For example, choosing to harm or choosing to help, just as they are different, they will be in line with the next step. Either positive soul progression or indeed not.

If you are awakening to your higher self you may find yourself not agreeing with people you once did, or becoming frustrated by others you assumed where on your path too. It is important to love yourself first as difficult as it may seem, not all will make the journey with you. Best to stay strong and trust God. Those whom you truly love will always be in your journey, today and forever.

Soul Journey

I was shown a dream at one stage about midway through my intense development which in total lasted five years. This is not to say we stop learning, new miracles and circumstances are always evolving, in fact every day is new and different. But like attending university I would say as in any long-term work a certain amount of compulsory training standards must be learnt and met. I would not want to offer my service to the public if I hadn't felt that I was being shown that it was the right time. So about three years into my development work I was given a vision and knowing of my soul journey. As I have already mentioned I was shown that I was on my last Earth life, along with my soul family, as indeed soul families always travel and stay together for eternity. One vision I was given was far ahead in the future, in a time when all my soul family are reunited in heaven and the spirit world. I was given a vision of a new dynasty of which my soul family would be part of. I was shown a gathering at a great castle, it was a dignified and highly important gathering of allies of similar soul dynasties. Many people I recognised whilst others I didn't, but all of the people there were of the same intention. In our dynasty my parents were king and queen warriors whilst us children and partners were all important princess and prince warriors, our children and one day their children adding to the dynasty. It is important to note that the people of these dynasties are all warriors and we will have a set mission given to us by the Divine God which will be against dishonesty and other evils in some format. Our soul's work doesn't end in this life, I have been shown that work continues in the next life. Our duty will be to fight and protect the truth of God's love, in some way, but we will all have our roles. I of course am grateful for this foresight and know that this work will begin alongside my soul family in the next life, which I find both exciting and comforting.

Spiritual Warfare

Evil of course is always present. It is manmade, yet real. I say manmade, because it needn't be here if humans didn't feed it. Never more powerful than God's love but certainly something that needs to be kept in check and of course for the honour of God. Where there is a person there is choice, where there is choice there is evil, and this will never, ever change. However, people can change, if they choose to and indeed many as already said are becoming enlightened. Spiritual warfare is constantly happening on this plain and on some plains over the spirit world, though not in the realms above realm four the one I call heaven, nor the realms up to God's high council. That is why it is called lower energy because it only happens in the lower realms and on earth. Still if you're lucky to go straight to the realm of heaven or paradise, you may still be called to work against the lower, darker energy as a spiritual warrior. We are well into the days of this spiritual evolution and are already giving out the energy expected of us to indeed make the world a better place. It is in our soul's best interest and the world's best interests to pursue this wholeheartedly now, making way for the least warfare, pain and damage to the environment in which we live.

The Divine God has shown me the workings of his realms down to the dissolution of an evil soul. At first, I was scared, even overwhelmed, by these visions but now I fear nothing, knowledge is strength and power. It was a rewarding day when my blinkers were off and I realised I won't be alone as I am a team, soul family, member. Suffice to say my development or training spiritually was tough for some years, but I learnt an awful lot to bring forward to help others. It was like everything is tested and I became a product of my training. In my dad's words you need to go through it to be safe and useful. Which is contentment or happiness to me.

Past Lives and Wicca

As my spiritual business took off, I began looking further into Wicca and paganism, as naturally both resonated with me for their love and connection to nature and cycles. The name Wicca comes from the word 'wise'. Wicca is by no means an evil way of life in fact it is quite the opposite. It is working with energies as mediums or witches do. Working with the power of crystals, herbs, nature, prayer and intention and the natural cycles of time as in the moon energies and transitions of the solar system. As a medium or witch this is most natural as I work with and see the energy of everything anyway. I found a new (or ancient) outlet and a focus point for my prayer work. When working with special herbs I found a surprising great relief from problems or energies which were pestering me. Powerful and magical. My new daily practice has enriched my life and happiness.

I had a problem deep in my soul an energy trapped which I didn't much like so using my crystal ball as a point of focus, I was able to see images of some past lives. I was shown that I was in fact abused and murdered by a priest who took power of my witchhood. I believe I was also executed on a stake as a witch in a further past life too. Of course some one of my ability to read energies would have been known as witch historically.

Not surprising that I would be drawn to other like-minded people in modern spiritual terms or nature-based witches. I am attuned to the energies of both born that way naturally. I love the symbols in Wicca, the most well known the pentagram the triangle and the star. Once deemed an evil sign of a witch, it in fact means Divine harmony and peace. Witches were widely misunderstood and hunted by priests even for sexual gain. Witches are in fact the epitome of nature and animal lovers, in tune with the message nature brings and its powers to heal and bring about positive change. I think the biggest challenge for a medium like myself is that you can't make anyone understand how it works or how witches are. Unless you are open and willing to understand. There are secrets that only the Divine God knows and keeps. I believe that why some are born a medium or witch and others not. Is one of those secrets.

People of my ability and gift are still not fully respected by any means, I am no different to another race, creed or culture who are persecuted in some way or another. The modern spiritual community like myself is here for a reason. To counteract prejudice for one and to bring back to the world the true reality of the magic of God's awesome love and energies, battered down over centuries by power, ego and prejudice. Now it is the time for people to realise these truths once more and there are Facebook groups etc of people of this ilk worldwide today, sharing their magic of nature, crystals and the elements and also good vibes. Making prayers for the world's disasters and joining forces the Divine God's power for good and abundance. Importantly I am here with other spiritualists all over the world not only to prove the existence of the vast heavenly realms but to give knowledge, impart God Divine's wisdom from the eyes of one who is shown and be a medium of Divine light and good intention for the world. There are sacred jobs which some spiritualists have, some work with dragon energies, some are experts in crystal healing alongside mediumship of other spiritual work. Every spiritual person is unique and unique in their abilities or gifts and unique in their work. I have a very strong desire for justice and morals. I believe in the banishing of evil spirits by the light and have been shown and told how this happens. I have also been of assistance in this by being shown such an evil dark spirit and demanding Divine light over it and watching it dissolve.

When we all reach the next life. I won't seem different as I do more so on Earth. Whether people believe now or not, there really is no questioning when we are in spirit ourselves. I've had a truly tough time on earth, but I honour what Divine God has made me to be. In this life and the next.

www.ingramcontent.com/pod-product-compliance
Lightning Source LLC
Chambersburg PA
CBHW021144020426
42331CB00005B/884